PreTime® Piano
Favorites

Primer Level

Beginning Reading

Arranged by

Nancy and Randall Faber

Production: Frank and Gail Hackinson
Production Coordinator: Marilyn Cole
Design and Illustration: Terpstra Design, San Francisco
Music Editor: Edwin McLean
Engraving: Tempo Music Press, Inc.
Montclair Music Studio
104 Watchung Avenue
Upper Montclair, NJ 0704
973-783-4330

FABER
PIANO ADVENTURES®
3042 Creek Drive
Ann Arbor, Michigan 48108

A NOTE TO TEACHERS

PreTime® Piano Favorites is a collection of familiar folk tunes well-loved by children. The purpose of *PreTime®* is to provide the earliest level of reading for the beginning pianist. No eighth notes or dotted rhythms are used, and the hands remain in Middle C position. Tasteful illustrations and use of color add to the charm of *PreTime®*.

PreTime® Piano Favorites is part of the *PreTime® Piano* series. "PreTime" designates the Primer Level of the *PreTime® to BigTime® Piano Supplementary Library* arranged by Faber and Faber.

Following are the levels of the supplementary library which lead from *PreTime®* to *BigTime®*.

PreTime® Piano	(Primer level)
PlayTime® Piano	(Level 1)
ShowTime® Piano	(Level 2A)
ChordTime® Piano	(Level 2B)
FunTime® Piano	(Level 3A – 3B)
BigTime® Piano	(Level 4)

Each level offers books in a variety of styles, making it possible for teachers to offer stimulating material for every student. For a complimentary detailed listing, e-mail faber@pianoadventures.com or write us at the mailing address below.

Visit **www.PianoAdventures.com**.

Teacher Duets

Optional teacher duets are a valuable feature of the *PreTime® Piano* series. Although the arrangements stand complete on their own, the duets provide a fullness of harmony and rhythmic vitality. And not incidentally, they offer the oppurtunity for parent and student to play together.

Helpful Hints:

1. The student should know his part thoroughly before the teacher duet is used. Accurate rhythm is especially important.
2. Rehearsal numbers are provided to give the student and teacher starting places.
3. The teacher may wish to count softly a measure aloud before beginning, as this will help the ensemble.

ISBN 978-1-61677-012-9

TABLE OF CONTENTS

Yankee Doodle 4

The Muffin Man 5

London Bridge 6

The Wheels on the Bus 7

Eensie Weensie Spider 8

Baa! Baa! Black Sheep 10

On the Bridge 12

Hush, Little Baby 13

Alouette 14

Shoo, Fly 16

Pop! Goes the Weasel 18

Row, Row, Row Your Boat 20

Music Dictionary 21

4

Yankee Doodle

Thumbs share Middle C

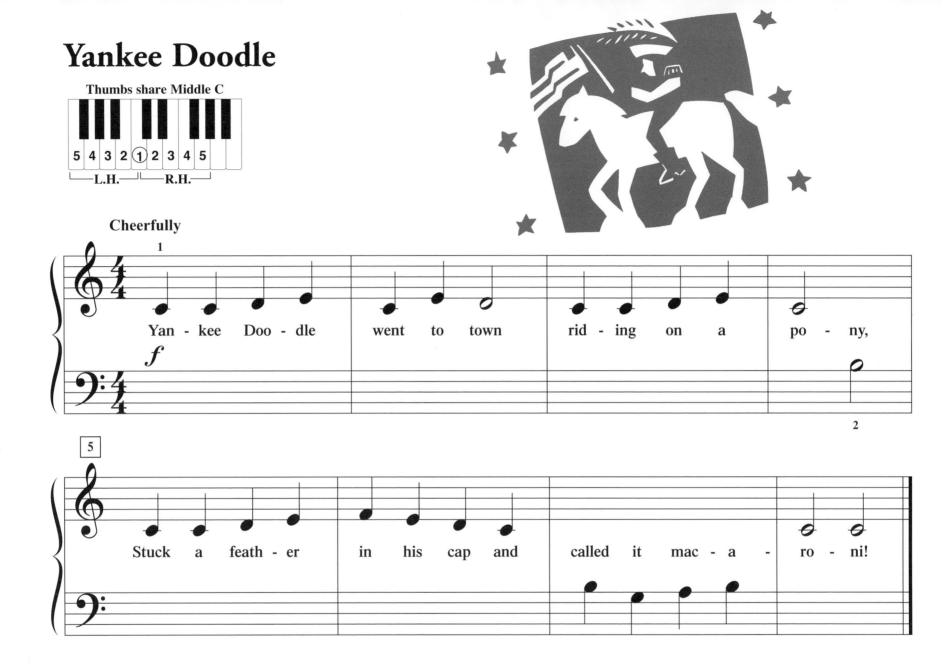

Cheerfully

Yan - kee Doo - dle | went to town | rid - ing on a | po - ny,

Stuck a feath - er | in his cap and | called it mac - a - | ro - ni!

Teacher Duet: (Student plays 1 octave higher)

The Muffin Man

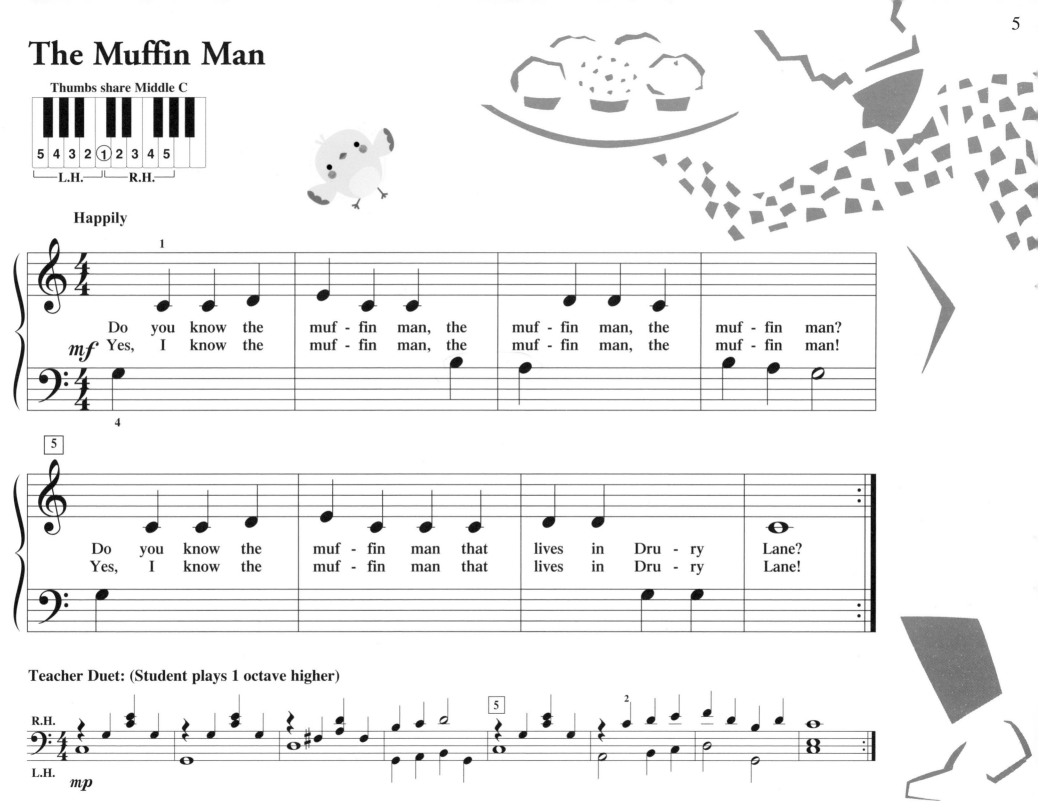

Thumbs share Middle C

Happily

Do you know the muf - fin man, the muf - fin man, the muf - fin man?
Yes, I know the muf - fin man, the muf - fin man, the muf - fin man!

Do you know the muf - fin man that lives in Dru - ry Lane?
Yes, I know the muf - fin man that lives in Dru - ry Lane!

Teacher Duet: (Student plays 1 octave higher)

London Bridge

Teacher Duet: (Student plays 1 octave higher)

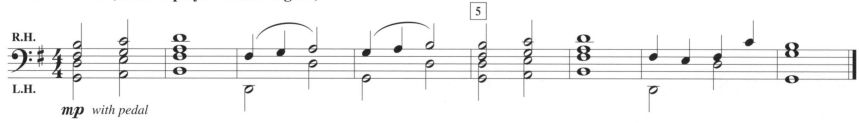

The Wheels on the Bus

Thumbs share Middle C

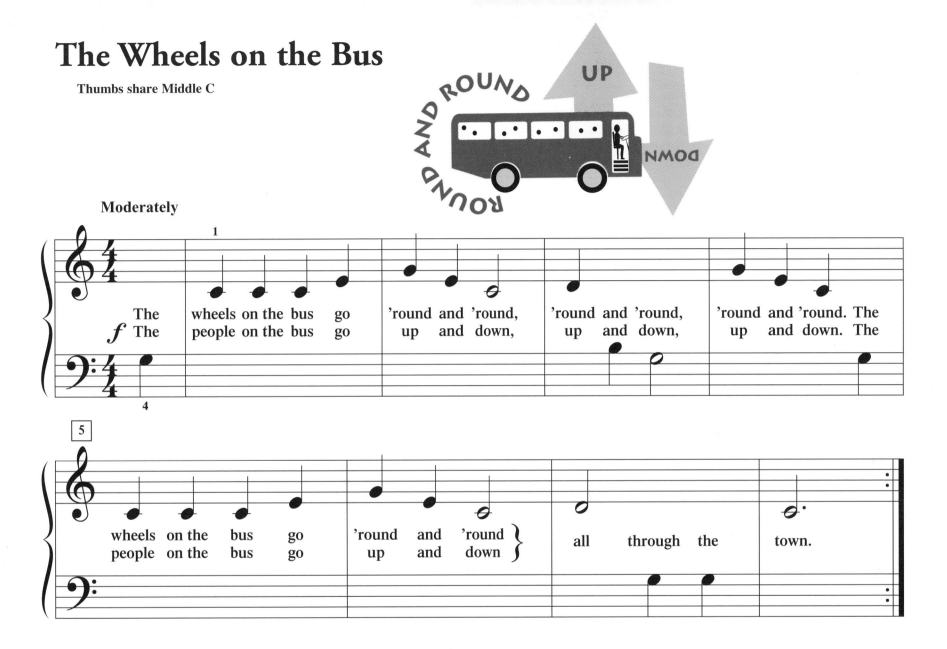

Moderately

The
The

wheels on the bus go
people on the bus go

'round and 'round,
up and down,

'round and 'round,
up and down,

'round and 'round. The
up and down. The

wheels on the bus go
people on the bus go

'round and 'round
up and down

all through the

town.

Teacher Duet: (Student plays 1 octave higher)

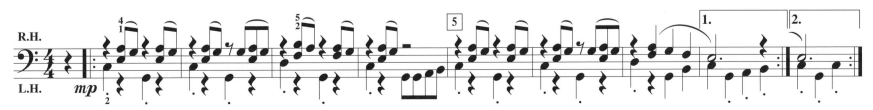

FF1012

8

Eensie Weensie Spider

C 5-Finger Scale

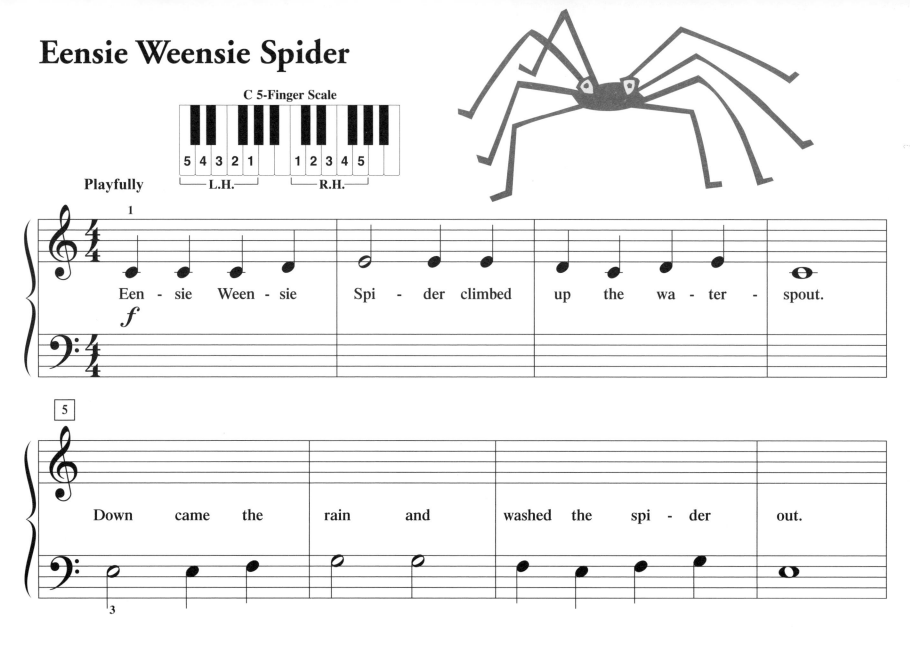

Playfully

Een - sie Ween - sie Spi - der climbed up the wa - ter - spout.

f

Down came the rain and washed the spi - der out.

Teacher Duet: (Student plays 1 octave higher)

R.H.

L.H.

mf

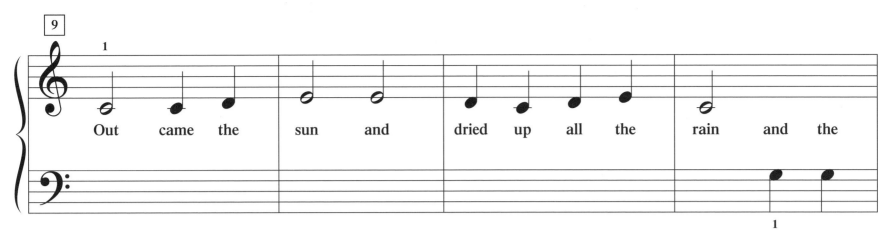

Out came the sun and dried up all the rain and the

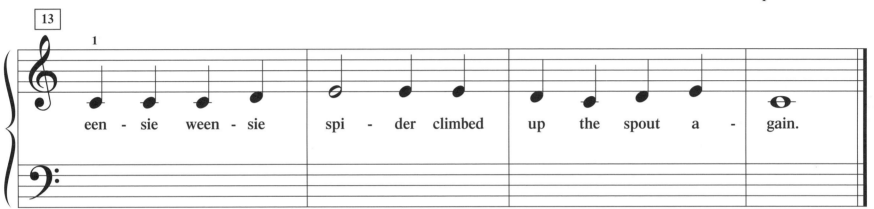

een - sie ween - sie spi - der climbed up the spout a - gain.

Baa! Baa! Black Sheep

Thumbs share Middle C

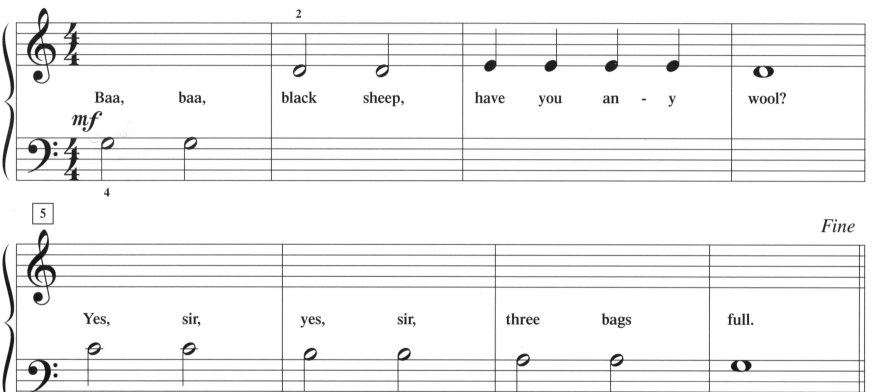

With motion

Baa, baa, black sheep, have you an - y wool?

Fine

Yes, sir, yes, sir, three bags full.

Teacher Duet: (Student plays 1 octave higher)

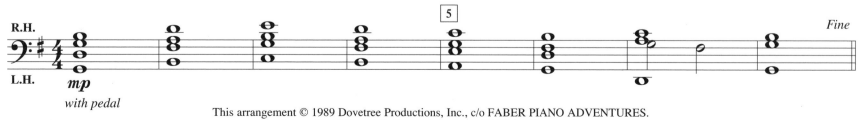

with pedal

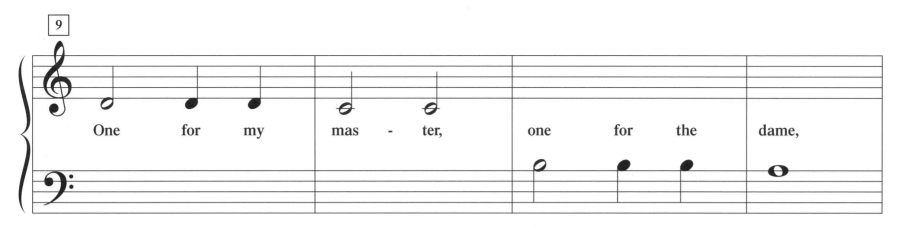

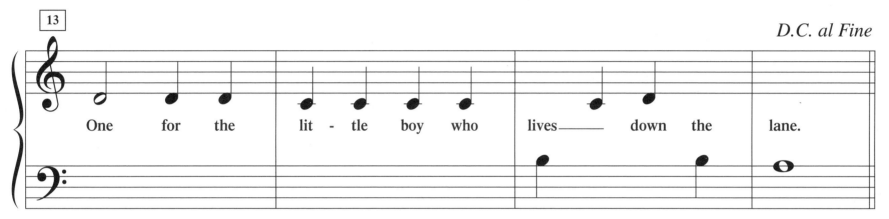

D.C. al Fine

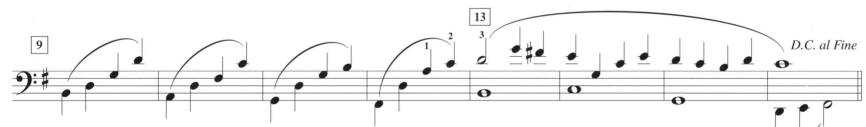

On the Bridge

Thumbs share Middle C

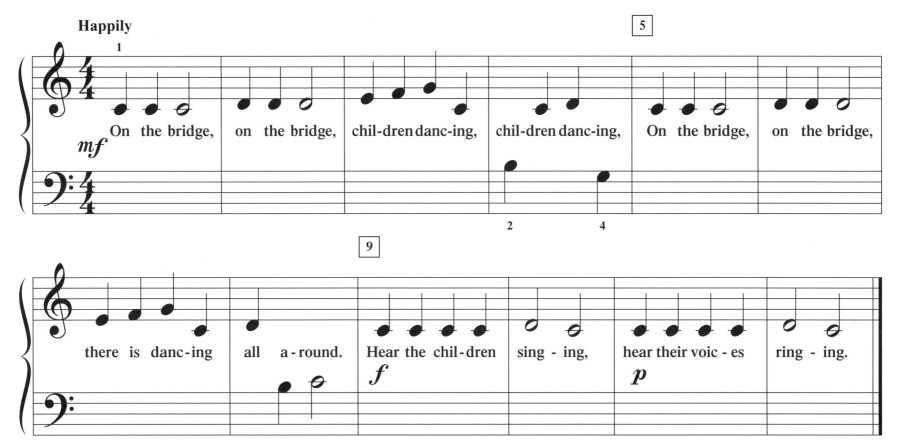

Teacher Duet: (Student plays 1 octave higher)

Hush, Little Baby

Thumbs share Middle C

Teacher Duet: (Student plays 1 octave higher)

Alouette

Thumbs share Middle C

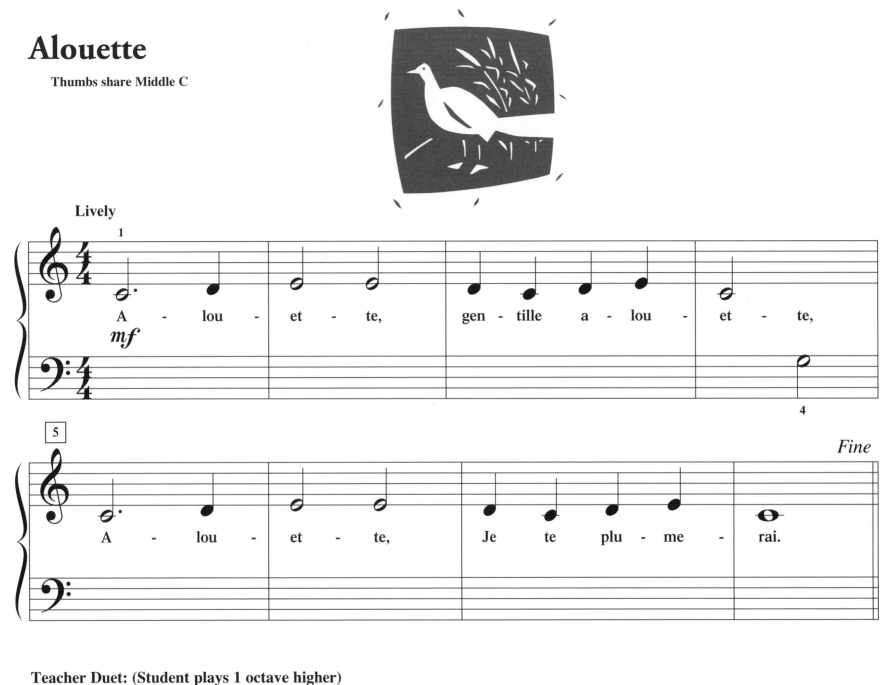

Lively

A - lou - et - te, gen - tille a - lou - et - te,

Fine

A - lou - et - te, Je te plu - me - rai.

Teacher Duet: (Student plays 1 octave higher)

Fine

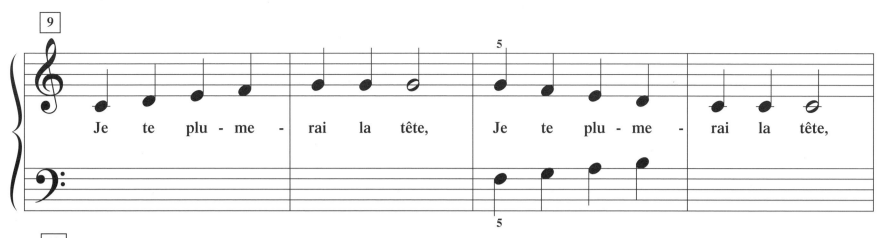

D.C. al Fine

Shoo, Fly

Thumbs share Middle C

With energy

Shoo, fly, don't both - er me, Shoo, fly, don't both - er me,

mf

Shoo, fly, don't both - er me, For I be - long to some - bod - y. I

Teacher Duet: (Student plays 1 octave higher)

R.H.

L.H.

mp

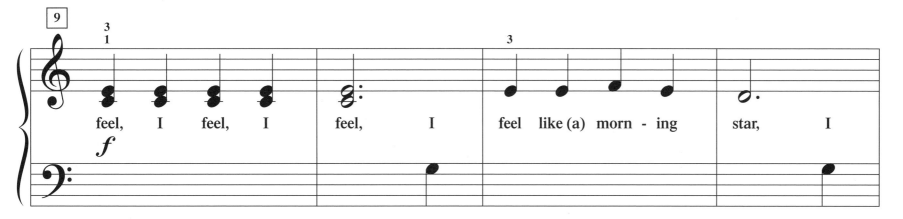

feel, I feel, I feel, I feel like (a) morn - ing star, I

feel, I feel, I feel, I feel like (a) morn - ing star.

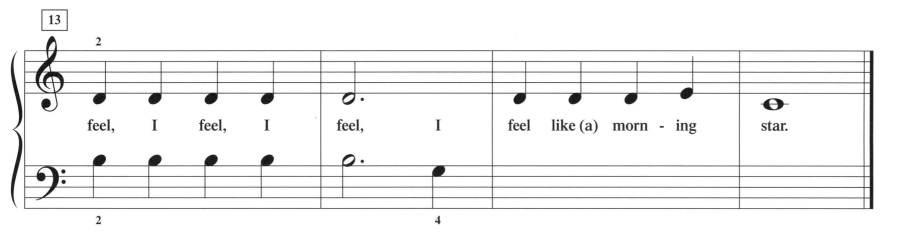

Pop! Goes the Weasel

Thumbs share Middle C

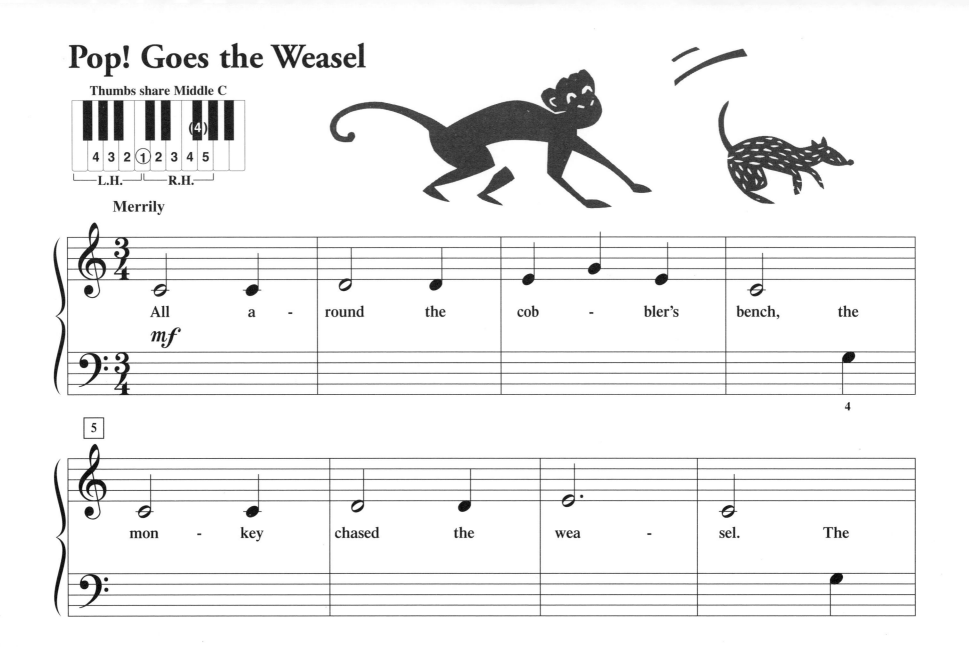

Merrily

All a - round the cob - bler's bench, the

mf

4

5 mon - key chased the wea - sel. The

Teacher Duet: (Student plays 1 octave higher)

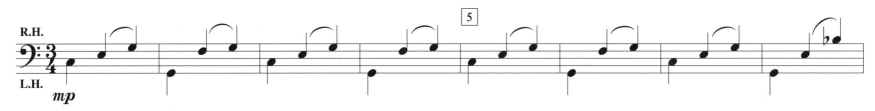

R.H.

5

L.H.

mp

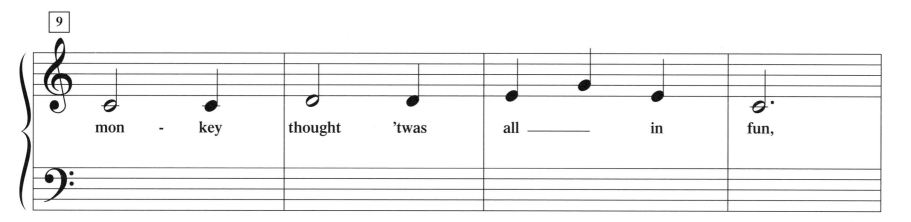

mon-key thought 'twas all —— in fun,

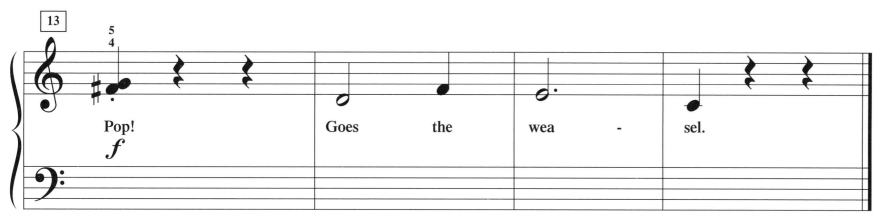

Pop! Goes the wea - sel.

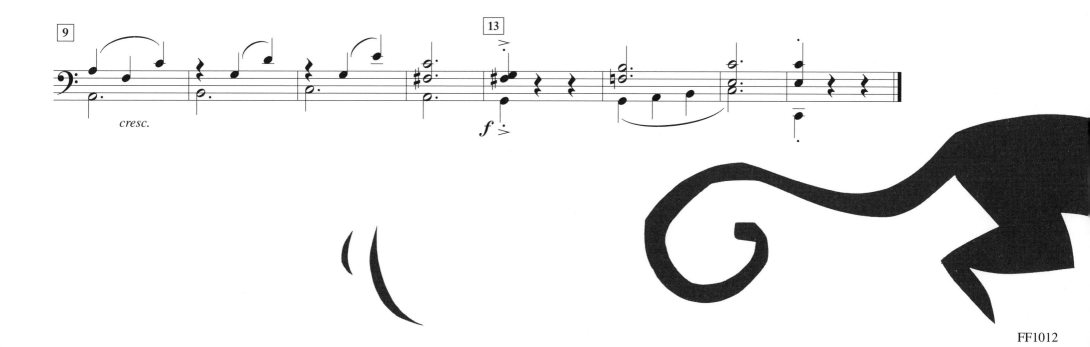

cresc.

Row, Row, Row Your Boat

Thumbs share Middle C

Playfully

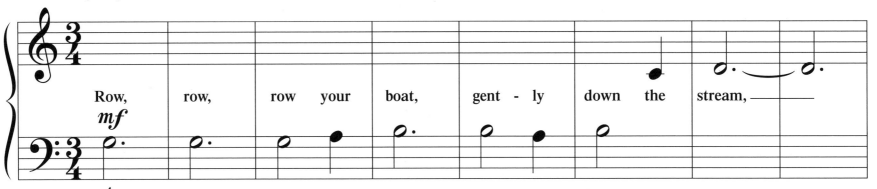

Row, row, row your boat, gent - ly down the stream,

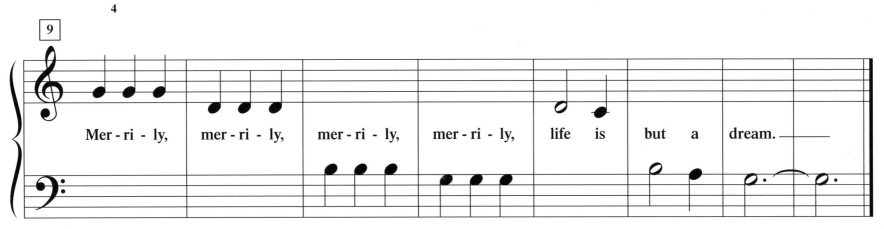

Mer - ri - ly, mer - ri - ly, mer - ri - ly, mer - ri - ly, life is but a dream.

Teacher Duet: (Student plays 1 octave higher)

R.H.

L.H.

This arrangement © 1989 Dovetree Productions, Inc., c/o FABER PIANO ADVENTURES.
International Copyright Secured.   All Rights Reserved.

FF1012